Surviving Floods

Elizabeth Raum

www.raintreepublishers.co.uk
Visit our website to find out more information about Raintree books.

To order:
☎ Phone 0845 6044371
🖷 Fax +44 (0) 1865 312263
🖳 Email myorders@raintreepublishers.co.uk

Customers from outside the UK please telephone +44 1865 312262

Raintree is an imprint of **Capstone Global Library Limited**, a company incorporated in England and Wales having its registered office at 7 Pilgrim Street, London, EC4V 6LB – Registered company number: 6695582

Edited by Louise Galpine and Laura Knowles
Designed by Victoria Allen
Original illustrations © Capstone Global Library Limited 2011
Illustrated by HLSTUDIOS
Picture research by Ruth Blair
Originated by Capstone Global Library Limited
Printed and bound in China by CTPS

ISBN 978 1 406 22214 2 (hardback)
15 14 13 12 11
10 9 8 7 6 5 4 3 2 1

British Library Cataloguing in Publication Data
Raum, Elizabeth.
Surviving floods. -- (Children's true stories. Natural disasters)
363.3'493-dc22
A full catalogue record for this book is available from the British Library.

Acknowledgements
We would like to thank the following for permission to reproduce photographs: © Corbis pp. **8**, **11**; Corbis pp. **5** (© HO/Reuters), **17** (© Brooks Kraft/Sygma), **18** (© Andrew Holbrooke), **19** (© Andrew Holbrooke), **23** (© Gideon Mendel for Action Aid), **24** (© RAFIQUR RAHMAN/Reuters), **26** (© STRINGER/epa); Getty Images pp. **4** (Carsten Koall), **14** (Topical Press Agency), **20** (Chris Wilkins/AFP), **21** (Joe Raedle); © Glenn Baker, Easy Like Water p. **25**; © Johnstown Area Heritage Association Archives p. **7**; Library of Congress p. **9** (George Barker); Superstock pp. **13** (© Science and Society), **15** (© The Francis Frith Collection).

Cover photograph of a girl carrying her sister on her shoulder wading through a water logged road through a suburb in Dhaka, Bangladesh, 19 September 2004 reproduced with permission of Corbis/© Rafiqur Rahman/Reuters.

Quotations on pages 7, 9, and 10 are from David G. McCullogh, *The Johnstown Flood*, Simon & Schuster, 1987. Quotation on page 8 is from Christine Gibson, "Our 10 Greatest Natural Disasters", *American Heritage* Magazine, August/September 2006, Volume 57, Issue 4. Mosa Rita's story on page 23 is from Helen Rowe, "Hope floats for Bangladeshi children on school boats" October 8, 2007, The *Brunei Times*.

The author would like to thank Richard Lord, Lindsey Pieper, and Mohammed Rezwan for so generously sharing their stories.

We would like to thank Daniel Block for his invaluable help in the preparation of this book.

Contents

DAILY LIFE

Read here to learn about what life was like for the children in these stories, and the impact the disaster had at home and school.

NUMBER CRUNCHING

Find out here the details about natural disasters and the damage they cause.

Survivors' lives

Read these boxes to find out what happened to the children in this book when they grew up.

HELPING HAND

Find out how people and organizations have helped to save lives.

On the scene

Read eyewitness accounts of the natural disasters in the survivors' own words.

Some words are printed in bold, **like this**. You can find out what they mean by looking in the glossary on page 30.

Introduction

A flood is when water covers land that is normally dry. When too much rain soaks an area, it causes rivers to rise and water pours out over land. Melting snow, high tides, hurricanes, and seasonal rains – such as Asia's **monsoon rains** – may cause floods. Some areas, called **flood plains**, flood every few years. Sometimes, floods occur in areas that have been dry for a hundred years or more.

Melting snow caused flooding in the town of Koenigstein, Germany in April 2006.

DAILY LIFE

Floods affect thousands of children every year. Some only just escape with their lives. Others watch as floodwater damages their homes and schools. Floods, like other natural disasters, can change lives forever.

NUMBER-CRUNCHING

It takes only about 15 centimetres (6 inches) of fast-moving water to knock a person down. A car begins to float in 60 centimetres (2 feet) of water.

Flash floods

Some floods happen slowly, trapping towns or villages as the water rises around them. **Flash floods** happen quickly, often without warning. Too much rain, melting snow, broken **dykes** or dams, high tides, or hurricanes can cause flash floods. People may be trapped in homes or cars by the rising water. Fast-moving water may float houses off their foundations or sweep cars into deep water.

The Cumberland River flooded areas of Tennessee, USA in May 2010, leaving 22 people dead and forcing thousands to leave their homes.

Johnstown, Pennsylvania, USA: 1889

In Johnstown, Pennsylvania, 30 May 1889 was a holiday. People went shopping and watched a parade. By the middle of the afternoon, it began to rain. More than 25 centimetres (10 inches) of rain fell on the nearby mountains. Rivers and lakes swelled.

Six-year-old Gertrude Quinn saw worry in her father's face. The South Fork Dam, built in 1852, was only 22 kilometres (14 miles) away from the town. If the dam were to burst, water would pour into Johnstown.

Key
Towns and villages
Mountains

Conemaugh River

South Forks

Mineral Point

South Forks Creek

Conemaugh

South Fork Dam

Railway line

Conemaugh Lake Reservoir

Woodvale

UNITED STATES Johnstown, Pennsylvania

N

Johnstown

0
0

5 miles
5 kilometres

This map shows the Johnstown area. When the South Fork Dam burst, floodwaters flowed down the Conemaugh River towards Johnstown.

DAILY LIFE

In 1889, there were no telephones, radios, or cars in Johnstown. Messages were delivered by hand. Many children spent the rainy day before the flood reading, doing chores, or playing board games.

Run!

The next morning, Mr Quinn ordered Gertrude to stay inside. But Gertrude disobeyed him. She sat on the porch and dipped her feet into the rainwater. Ducks swam by. Just before 4.00 p.m., her father came home from work. As he was telling Gertrude off, he heard a rushing noise.

Mr Quinn saw a wall of water rushing towards Johnstown. "Run for your lives," he shouted. The dam had burst.

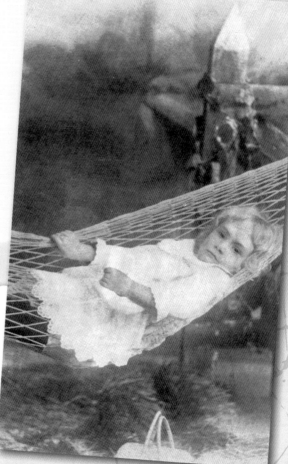

This photo of Gertrude was taken before the Johnstown flood.

Disaster

Gertrude's father carried one of Gertrude's sisters. Her other sister was big enough to walk through the water. Libby Hipp, their 18-year-old nanny, carried Gertrude. Gertrude's Aunt Abbie, who was visiting, carried her own baby. But as the water rose higher and higher, Aunt Abbie was afraid. She turned back. So did Libby.

After the flood, people combed through the damaged buildings trying to find anything of value.

On the scene

Victor Heiser, aged 16, was in Johnstown on the day of the flood. He later wrote, "I could see a huge wall advancing with incredible **rapidity** down the diagonal street. It was not recognizable as water, it was a dark mass in which **seethed** houses, **freight cars**, trees, and animals."

Separated

Gertrude kicked and screamed, calling "Papa, Papa!" But it was too late. Papa was on the hill, and Gertrude was back at the house with Libby and Aunt Abbie. As Mr Quinn watched from the hillside, the house – with Gertrude inside – rocked back and forth, tipped over, and disappeared into the rushing waters.

The flood destroyed hundreds of homes and left about 25,000 people homeless.

NUMBER CRUNCHING

Around 2,200 people died in the flood. That was 1 out of every 10 people who lived in Johnstown.

Swept away

When the house tipped into the river, Gertrude fell on to a muddy mattress floating in the water. She yelled for help. A mill worker named Maxwell McArchren jumped from a nearby rooftop onto the mattress. Another man, in the window of a nearby house, called, "Throw that baby over here!"

McArchren tossed Gertrude 3–4.5 metres (10–15 feet) across the water. Luckily, someone caught her! Gertrude was so frightened that she didn't say a word until her father found her the next day. Gertrude was lucky. Many others died, including Libby Hipp, Aunt Abbie, and her baby.

HELPING HAND

The Johnstown flood was the first major disaster dealt with by the American Red Cross. Clara Barton, who founded the Red Cross in 1881, spent five months in Johnstown setting up hospitals, kitchens, and emergency housing. People from across the United States and 14 other countries sent money and supplies.

Rebuilding

After the waters **receded**, Mr Quinn sent Gertrude to stay with relatives in Pittsburgh, about 120 kilometres (75 miles) away. Many others left, too. However, like Gertrude, they returned when homes and schools were rebuilt. The survivors never forgot the Johnstown flood. It changed their lives forever.

After the flood, people lived in caves, tents, or huts built of scraps until they could rebuild their houses.

North Sea Floods, UK: 1953

Saturday, 31 January 1953 was a cold, clear night in the towns along the coast of the North Sea. People enjoyed their usual activities. They had no idea that a gigantic flood was on the way.

This map shows the land that flooded on 31 January 1953. Strong winds sent seawater into towns and cities along both North Sea coasts.

Richard's story

Seven-year-old Richard Lord lived in the seaside town of Felixstowe (see map on page 12). That evening, Richard and his parents went to the cinema. They stopped for fish and chips on the way home, and then Richard went to bed.

Around midnight, Richard's parents rushed into his room. They woke him up. The water in his room was already waist deep. Richard was scared. He couldn't swim.

Richard's father lifted him on to the roof. Both parents joined him. They spent the night huddled on the roof as water rose around them.

This photo, taken from the air, shows how the flooding turned streets and fields into lakes.

On the scene

Richard remembers the night of the flood. "We lay on the roof, my parents on either side of me to keep me warm. Although I was frightened, I remember seeing everything happening. It was still clear and bright, but a very strong wind blew through the night. Although I was obviously dozing off and coming round it was very, very cold."

Rescuers used rowing boats to check houses and take people to safety.

Rescue

Throughout the night Richard heard neighbours scream, and he saw trees, pieces of houses, and even a cow float past. Floodwaters lifted the house off its foundations and carried it away for several streets.

The next morning, rescuers in rowing boats carried Richard and his family to dry land. Richard didn't learn until later that several of his friends had not survived.

HELPING HAND

Richard believes his parents saved his life that night. "I lay between them both to keep warm from their body heat. Without them, I would have died."

Preventing more disasters

Strong winds sent water from the North Sea pouring into towns along the English coast. The same storm also caused death and destruction in the Netherlands.

After the 1953 flood, both England and the Netherlands built barriers made of concrete and steel along the coasts. In England, engineers rebuilt beaches of sand or loose rocks in front of these **seawalls**. The beaches break the force of the waves. This protects the seawalls, which then hold back the water.

On Canvey Island, England, a sandy beach in front of a seawall helps prevent flooding.

NUMBER CRUNCHING

This chart shows how many people died and how much damage was caused by the North Sea Floods.

	Eastern England	The Netherlands
Deaths	307	1,835
Houses damaged	around 24,000	around 46,000
Land flooded	728 square kilometres (281 square miles)	1,305 square kilometres (504 square miles)

Mississippi River, USA: 1993

The Mississippi River has been flooding for thousands of years. As melting snow and summer rains swell the river, it flows into the nearby **wetlands**. The wetlands act like sponges, soaking up the extra water.

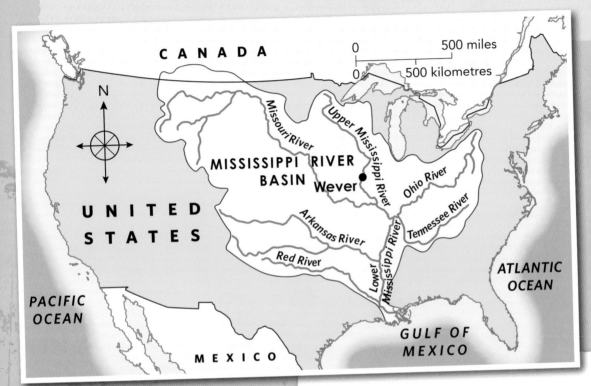

Several major rivers drain into the Mississippi River, leading to flooding during the spring and summer.

Record rains

When people began settling along the Mississippi River, they turned the wetlands into farms, towns, and cities. To protect against flooding, they built **levees** to hold the river back. These usually worked. But in 1993, record amounts of rain fell. Nothing could hold back the Mighty Mississippi or the 150 rivers and **tributaries** that join with the Mississippi to form the world's third-largest **river basin**.

HELPING HAND

When the Mississippi River began to burst through its levees and threatened to overflow, whole communities joined together to build sandbag dykes to hold the water back. Thousands of people filled bags with sand and stacked them up to form dykes. Older children helped fill sandbags. Younger children delivered food and drinks to the volunteers.

These volunteers are building sandbag dykes near Des Moines, Iowa, USA.

NUMBER-CRUNCHING

Rivers involved	150
Days flood lasted	200 days in some locations
US states involved	9
Total land area involved	1,036,000 square kilometres (400,000 square miles)
Farmlands flooded	60,700 square kilometres (23,440 square miles)
Failed levees	1,000
Towns completely flooded	75
Homes destroyed	10,000
Deaths	50

Lindsey's story

In 1993, eight-year-old Lindsey Pieper lived on a large farm in Wever, Iowa, USA (see map on page 16). There were 35 kilometres (22 miles) of levees surrounding the farm to protect it from the river, which was 3.2 kilometres (2 miles) away. If the levees broke, the farm would flood.

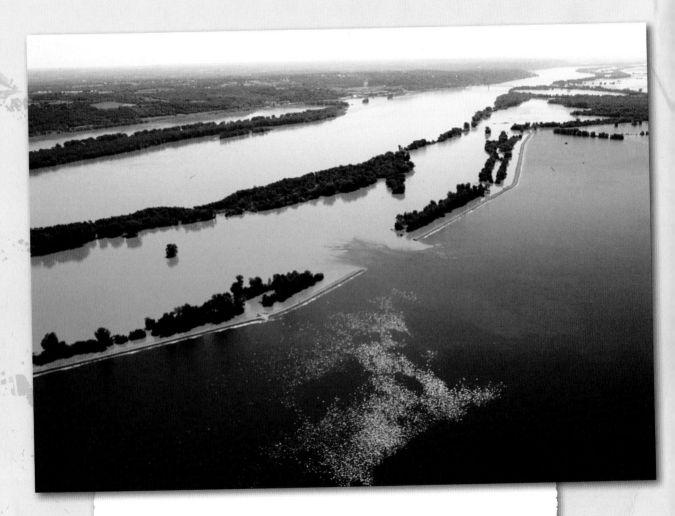

When the levees broke, the Mississippi River overflowed its banks and flooded nearby farms and towns.

Preparing for disaster

In July, Lindsey's dad told everyone to prepare for a flood. Lindsey was worried. What did he mean?

The family packed clothing and supplies. Friends came to help move heavy furniture to the first floor of the farmhouse, and volunteers worked day and night to repair and rebuild failing levees. Lindsey carried food and drinks to them.

Despite their efforts, the levees leaked. The day before they broke, Lindsey's family moved into town. They stayed in a crowded hotel room for two weeks. Lindsey was safe and dry, but she worried about the future.

The Mississippi River flowed into farm fields and buildings.

HELPING HAND

Lindsey's parents spent time explaining the situation to their children. "If we had questions or were scared, they made us feel comfortable," Lindsey says. Most importantly, they made sure the children were safe both before and after the farm flooded.

The mess

After the waters began to recede, Lindsey and her family returned to the farm by boat. "The house smelled awful," Lindsey remembers. The ground floor walls were wet and crumbling, and dead fish lay on the floor.

This photo shows a coast guard boat travelling though the city centre of a town in Iowa that was also flooded by the Mississippi River.

HELPING HAND

Many volunteer groups helped to rebuild the Piepers' home. Whenever she sits on the front porch, Lindsey remembers the church group that rebuilt it. Laura, a teenage volunteer, took time to play and joke with Lindsey.

The clean-up operation

Cleaning up after a flood was a big job. Many houses and buildings had to be taken down. Schools and hospitals were damaged. So were 10 airports. Trains and river barges stopped moving for several weeks.

In many homes, the entire ground floor, including furniture, flooring, and walls, was destroyed.

Lindsey's life now

Lindsey's family still lives on the farm in Wever, Iowa. In 2008, the Mississippi River flooded again. Lindsey, who is now a university student, was in charge of supplying food and drinks to volunteer flood fighters. Her entire family wanted to help others as they had been helped in 1993.

Bangladesh: 2007

In 2007, monsoon rains flooded many areas of Bangladesh. In some areas, floods occur yearly. In the hilly areas of northeastern Bangladesh, rivers overflow each spring and autumn. Melting **glaciers** in the Himalayan mountains send floodwaters into the valleys.

Most of Bangladesh is very flat, with many rivers. Every year, the River Ganges and other major rivers carry melting snow from the Himalayan mountains into towns and villages.

NUMBER-CRUNCHING

In Bangladesh in 2007, two major floods destroyed 337 schools and damaged around 5,000 others.

Mosa's story

Mosa Rita, who was seven years old in 2007, spent her days as a housemaid. She cleaned and cooked for another family in her village in the Natore district of Bangladesh (see map on page 22). Her father was a fisherman. Her family relied on the money that Mosa earned as a maid.

Hard work has always been part of Mosa's life. So are floods. But it is not easy. Schools close for about four months of each year due to floods.

Happily for Mosa Rita, architect Mohammed Rezwan has a solution: floating schools.

These children, who lost their homes in the 2007 flood, are queuing for a bowl of rice.

Floating schools

During the 2007 floods, Mosa Rita went to school on a boat. Every evening at 6.30 p.m., the school boat picked her up on the riverbank. She left school at 9.00 p.m. "The teachers teach us very well," she said. Education makes her future brighter.

Getting to school during floods is difficult because the streets are filled with floodwater.

Mohammed Rezwan

When Mohammed Rezwan was a boy, **seasonal floods** closed his school. The problem of closed schools always bothered him. In 2002, he developed a solution. He designed boats as classrooms. These boats are fitted with multi-layered waterproof roofs. The boats use **solar power** to run lights and computers. Solar lights allow students to study after dark. Rezwan plans to add more floating schools, libraries, and even hospitals.

"I believe that if children cannot come to school then the school should go to them," Rezwan has said. He has received many awards for his great idea.

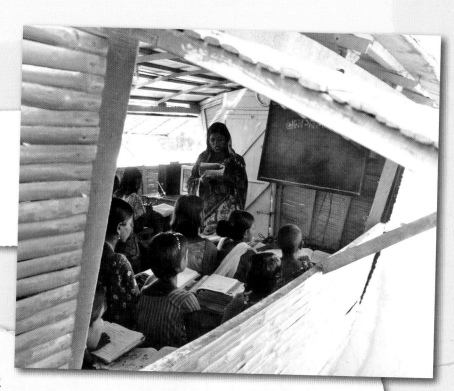

Floating schools allow children to attend school even during floods.

On the scene

"When we attend the boat school, we enjoy ourselves," a nine-year-old girl called Shakila Khatoon said in Bengali, the national language. "It's different from other schools."

Conclusion

It is impossible to prevent all floods. Rain, melting snow, and high **tides** are part of nature. But **engineers** have worked hard to protect cities and towns from repeated flooding. **Levees** and other barriers help to keep rivers under control. **Dams** are checked regularly, so they are less likely to burst. **Seawalls**, like the ones in eastern England and in the Netherlands, protect coastal towns and villages.

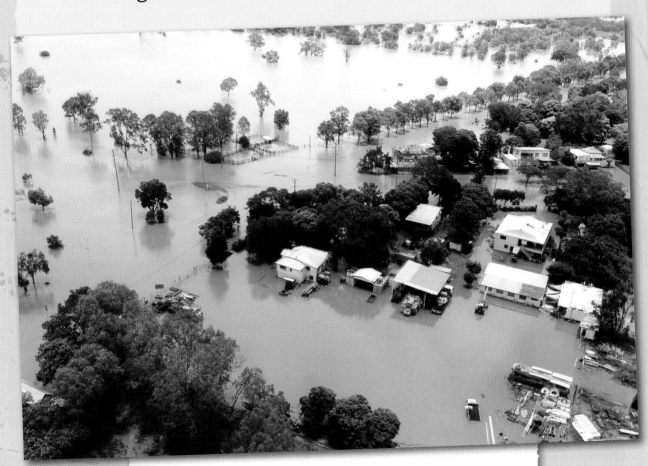

Tropical storms led to severe flooding in the Australian states of Queensland and Victoria in December 2010 and January 2011. Huge areas of land were flooded, affecting around 200,000 people.

HELPING HAND

Today, weather satellites help forecasters predict floods before they happen. Flood warnings appear on television, radio, and the internet. If people know a flood is expected, they can move to safety before the waters reach them.

Climate change

The floods in Bangladesh are made worse by our changing climate. As Earth gets warmer, glaciers like the ones high in the Himalayas melt. This sends more water into the already high rivers. **Global warming** also causes the sea to rise. This floods low-lying coastal areas.

Saving forests and wetlands

Floods also become more likely when forests are cut down. Forests prevent floods in several ways. Tree roots absorb water, and leaves protect the soil from heavy rains. This prevents erosion (washing away of the soil). Saving forests helps to prevent floods.

Wetlands act as "sponges" during floods, preventing floodwaters from spreading so far or fast. Most dams and dykes stop rivers from spreading out to the wetlands. This means that when floods occur, they may be even more **severe**. Today engineers are building better types of dams and dykes that protect wetlands and forests, as well as people. In the future, these new kinds of dams will help prevent damage from major floods.

Mapping floods

Floods can occur anywhere at anytime, especially after heavy rains. People living along seacoasts and major rivers are most likely to experience flooding.

Johnstown, Pennsylvania, USA

Flash floods, like the one that destroyed Johnstown, Pennsylvania in 1889, may occur when a dam or levee breaks. Today, dams are checked often and repaired when necessary.

Mississippi River, USA

When the Mississippi River overflowed in 1993, floodwaters destroyed thousands of homes and businesses. Restoring wetlands along rivers and coastlines helps prevent seasonal flooding.

NORTH AMERICA

Mississippi Drainage Basin

•Johnstown, Pennsylvania

ATLANTIC OCEAN

PACIFIC OCEAN

SOUTH AMERICA

England and the Netherlands

In 1953, heavy rains and high waves flooded coastal towns in England and the Netherlands. Hurricanes and tropical storms are a constant threat in coastal areas.

ENGLAND
Felixstowe **NETHERLANDS**
EUROPE

ASIA

AFRICA

BANGLADESH
Natore

PACIFIC OCEAN

INDIAN OCEAN

AUSTRALASIA

Bangladesh

Flooding in Bangladesh is increasing as Earth's climate changes. Small children, old people, and the poor are most likely to die during natural disasters such as floods or hurricanes.

ANTARCTICA

Glossary

dyke bank built to control or hold back the water of the sea or a river

flash flood flood that happens quickly, often without warning, usually caused by heavy rain, melting snows, high tides, or hurricanes

flood plain nearly flat plain along the course of a stream or river that is naturally likely to flood

freight car train carriage designed to carry cargo

glacier huge mass of ice formed by compacted snow that slowly flows over a landmass

global warming gradual rising of the Earth's temperature

levee dyke formed from earth, designed to prevent the flooding of a river

monsoon rain rains that fall during the rainy season in Bangladesh, India, and nearby lands

rapidity extreme quickness

recede go away or withdraw

river basin land area that is drained by a river and the streams that flow into it

seasonal flood flood that happens around the same time every year

seawall strong wall designed to prevent flooding from the sea

seethe surge or foam as if boiling

severe extremely bad

solar power energy from the sun

tributary stream that flows to a larger stream or other body of water

wetland land that has a wet and spongy soil, such as a marsh, swamp, or bog

Find out more

Books

Flood (Wild Weather), Catherine Chambers (Heinemann Library, 2008)

Raging Floods (Awesome Forces of Nature), Louise and Richard Spilsbury (Raintree, 2010)

Tsunamis and Floods (Graphic Natural Disasters), Gary Jeffrey (Franklin Watts, 2010)

Websites

www.bbc.co.uk/schools/whatisweather
Find out more about weather at this BBC website.

www.worldweather.org
The World Meteorological Organization website gives official weather observations and forecasts from all around the world.

www.esa.int/esaKIDSen/SEMD0LXJD1E_Earth_0.html
This is the European Space Agency's website for children, giving information about floods.

www.weatherwizkids.com/weather-rain.htm
The Weather WizKids website has flood information, plus all kinds of other weather facts.

Index